Dear Melanie,

We received your contact information from Jenny Jung at Michaels. We are excited to submit our products to you. Our target market are teens and adults.

Included in this package are Color Mi Vida - Coloring books "JOURNEY" and "HAPPY HOUR," along with their matching tote bags that can also be colored with fabric paint. The tote bags can read **Michaels.com** or and can display any of our 84 original designs.

ABOUT US:
Both of us, Erie & Rain (Erica & Renata) are mothers, artists, best friends & sisters. We are inspired by life, our children, our families and all human kind. All 84 pages are freehand and from the heart. "Journey" was created in 30 days, all while nursing our children. We have a natural passion to create, coupled with a natural talent to draw, our goal is to contribute these gifts to all that will accept. We wanted to see if there is a manner to distribute our coloring books through you, or work together and create a unique series to your company.

We are proud members of 1%ForThePlanet www.onepercentfortheplanet.org
This especially attracts millennial customers.

We truly appreciate your time,
Renata "Rain" Felix
e. Rain@ColorMiVida.com w. ColorMiVida.com t: 805-535-9907

Coloring takes us to a place of meditation, childhood, peace, creativity, coloring is art...
Art Inspires. Art Heals. ™

ColorMiVida.com